A Kid's Guide to

GL🌐BAL WARMING

How it affects you and what you can do about it.

Conceived and produced by Weldon Owen Pty Ltd
61 Victoria Street, McMahons Point
Sydney, NSW 2060, Australia

Copyright © 2008 Weldon Owen Pty Ltd
First printed 2008

Group Chief Executive Officer John Owen
President and Chief Executive Officer Terry Newell
Publisher Sheena Coupe
Creative Director Sue Burk
Vice President, International Sales Stuart Laurence
Vice President, Sales and New Business Development Amy Kaneko
Vice President, Sales: Asia and Latin America Dawn Low
Administrator, International Sales Kristine Ravn
Publishing Coordinator Mike Crowton

Managing Editor Jennifer Losco
Editor Helen Flint
Designer Gabrielle Green
Art Buyer Trucie Henderson

This edition created exclusively for Barnes & Noble, Inc.
ISBN-13: 978-1-4351-0591-1
ISBN-10: 1-4351-0591-5

Color reproduction by Chroma Graphics (Overseas) Pte Ltd
Printed in Malaysia by Tien Wah Press Pte Ltd

This book is printed on paper harvested from forests managed
with sustainable and environmentally sound practices.

A WELDON OWEN PRODUCTION

A Kid's Guide to
GLOBAL
WARMING

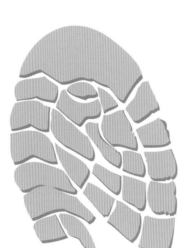

Glenn
Murphy

WELDON OWEN

Contents

6

What is global warming?

20
What does it mean for us?

36
What are we doing?

48
What can you do?

Power plant pollution Scientists believe that human activities are causing Earth to get warmer. When we burn fuel in power plants to create energy, we also create gases that trap heat from the Sun inside our atmosphere.

What is global warming?

Getting warmer faster

Earth was formed about 4.6 billion years ago and its temperature has changed through history. It has been warmer in the past than it is today, and sometimes much colder. But it is the speed at which Earth is now heating up that is alarming. For the first time in history, humans, not nature, are the main cause of Earth's changing climate —or, as it is commonly known, global warming.

Ice ages For long periods of time—called ice ages—Earth's surface was almost completely covered with ice. Much of the ice was stored in glaciers, such as this one in Antarctica.

Ice core Scientists study Earth's climate history by drilling ice cores out of ice sheets in Antarctica. They examine bubbles of ancient air inside the ice.

On the rise

When we burn fuel, gases are released, or emitted, into the atmosphere. Our gas emissions have been on the rise since the 1800s, when people started burning coal in factories to produce power. As emissions have increased, so has Earth's temperature.

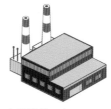

1882 First large electricity station

1908 First big discovery of oil in the Middle East

1913 First mass-produced motor car, the Model-T Ford

Average global temperature

1850   1860   1870   1880   1890   1900   1910   1920

Earth is warmer now than at any time in the past 1,000 years.

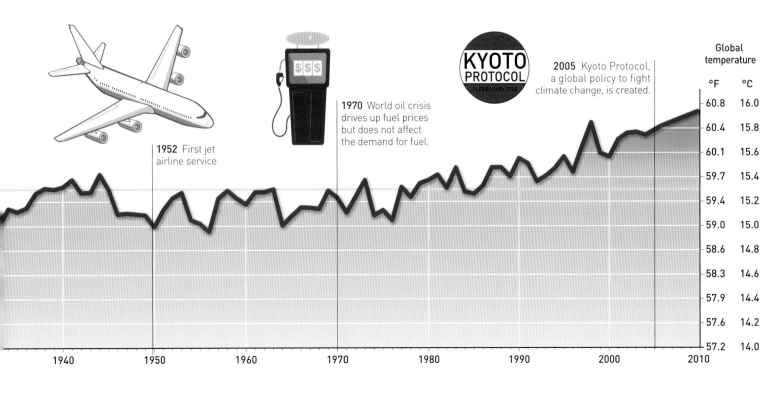

1952 First jet airline service

1970 World oil crisis drives up fuel prices but does not affect the demand for fuel.

KYOTO PROTOCOL
16 FEBRUARY 2005

2005 Kyoto Protocol, a global policy to fight climate change, is created.

Global temperature

°F	°C
60.8	16.0
60.4	15.8
60.1	15.6
59.7	15.4
59.4	15.2
59.0	15.0
58.6	14.8
58.3	14.6
57.9	14.4
57.6	14.2
57.2	14.0

1940 1950 1960 1970 1980 1990 2000 2010

Fossil fuels

All living things use and store carbon. Millions of years ago, when plants and animals died, some were buried, crushed, and fossilized under the ground. Oil, coal, and natural gas are formed from these fossilized remains —this is why they are called fossil fuels. When we burn fossil fuels we release large amounts of carbon into the atmosphere as part of the gas carbon dioxide (CO_2). It is released naturally from sources such as volcanoes, but humans and the machines we use are producing more CO_2 than ever before.

70% of the world's energy comes from burning fossil fuels.

Coal mining Coal is found in layers under the ground called seams. When we burn coal, the carbon that was stored inside the coal is released back into the atmosphere as carbon dioxide.

How coal is formed

Peat

Brown coal

Black coal

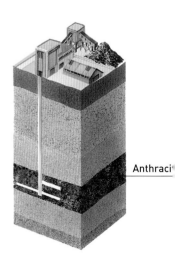

Anthracite

Forest life Millions of years ago, the remains of plants and animals in wet swampy forests were buried by sand, mud, and other plants. They formed a watery fuel called peat.

Brown coal The peat was buried in sediment and the weight of the rock pressing down on the peat squeezed out any water and gas. Slowly it compressed and fossilized into coal.

Black coal With more pressure and heat, the carbon in the coal was concentrated and the coal turned black. We mine black coal to fuel electric power stations.

Anthracite Anthracite is the highest grade of coal and can be almost pure carbon. We mine it for heating fuel. It forms when peat is subjected to heat and pressure over a long time.

Drilling at sea This enormous oil rig is being built off the coast of Norway. When it is finished, the oil rig will house all the workers and machinery needed to drill down and pump oil and natural gas that are trapped under the seafloor.

How oil and gas are formed

Dead sea creatures

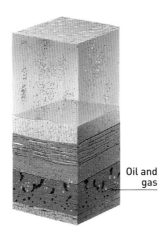

Oil and gas

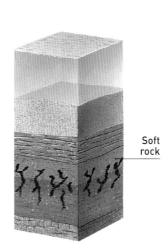

Soft rock

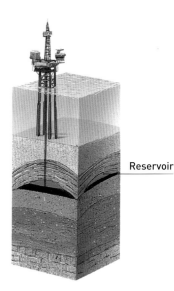

Reservoir

Ocean life When ancient sea creatures died they fell to the ocean floor. Over millions of years their bodies were covered by sand and mud that pressed together and eventually formed rock.

Oil and gas As this rock continued to pile up on top of the dead creatures, the crushing pressure fossilized their remains and turned them into oil and gas.

Rising up The oil and gas rose up through soft rock, but became trapped when they reached solid layers of rock, such as shale, that they could not pass through.

Drilling down Trapped under the solid rock, the oil and gas collected in a reservoir, with the gas on top of the oil. Rigs drill down and remove oil and gas to use as fuel.

Greenhouse gases

Greenhouse gases absorb heat from the Sun and help warm the planet, which makes it possible for plants and animals to live. Most greenhouse gases are a natural part of life. For example, humans breathe out small amounts of carbon dioxide into the air. But human activities have caused some gases to build up too much. Many scientists believe this increase in greenhouse gases is causing global warming.

What are greenhouse gases?

Carbon dioxide (CO_2) makes up more than 99 percent of the greenhouse gases in Earth's atmosphere. The remaining 0.6 percent contains methane, nitrous oxide, ozone, and halocarbons.

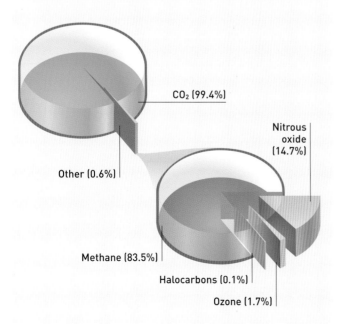

CO_2 (99.4%)

Other (0.6%)

Nitrous oxide (14.7%)

Methane (83.5%)

Halocarbons (0.1%)

Ozone (1.7%)

The carbon cycle

Carbon flows between land, sea, and sky in a natural cycle. But human activities are adding so much carbon to the atmosphere that these natural cycles have been thrown off balance.

Plant–atmosphere cycle
As they grow, plants trap and store huge amounts of carbon. They release only a little as they decay. This keeps CO_2 levels in Earth's atmosphere stable.

Ocean–atmosphere cycle
Marine plants, algae, and bacteria trap CO_2 in oceans and release it slowly as they grow. Some CO_2 also dissolves in and out of the ocean.

Burning fossil fuels
When we burn coal, gas, or oil, millions of years' worth of stored carbon enters the atmosphere in seconds. This extra carbon disrupts the natural cycle.

The greenhouse effect

The greenhouse effect is a natural process discovered in 1896. It has kept our planet warm enough to support life for billions of years. But as the amount of greenhouse gases increases, more heat is trapped in the atmosphere. The natural process has sped up and Earth is getting hotter.

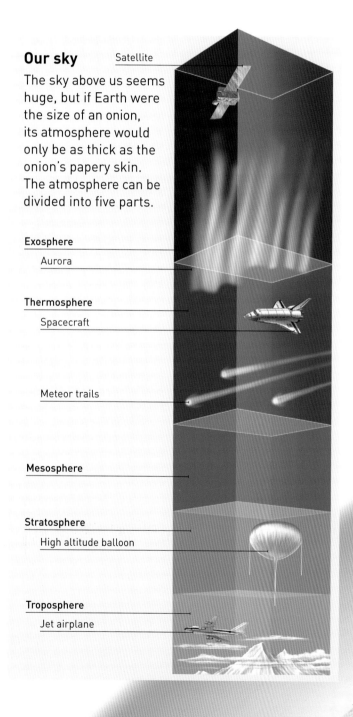

Our sky

The sky above us seems huge, but if Earth were the size of an onion, its atmosphere would only be as thick as the onion's papery skin. The atmosphere can be divided into five parts.

Satellite

Exosphere

Aurora

Thermosphere

Spacecraft

Meteor trails

Mesosphere

Stratosphere

High altitude balloon

Troposphere

Jet airplane

Life in a greenhouse

Just as the glass of a greenhouse lets in light and traps warm air inside, the greenhouse gases in Earth's atmosphere let sunlight pass through and trap heat inside.

Solar energy Only about half of the Sun's energy makes it to Earth's surface. The rest is bounced back or trapped by clouds and the atmosphere itself.

25%
is the amount CO₂
levels have increased
in the atmosphere
since 1850.

Solar rays Rays from
the Sun carry heat
and light to Earth.

Ice mirror Shiny
surfaces of Earth,
such as ice, bounce
4 percent of the Sun's
rays back into space.

Warm surface As the Sun's
rays warm the planet, the
surface of Earth gives off
heat. Some heat escapes into
space but greenhouse gases
in the atmosphere trap the
rest and make Earth warmer.

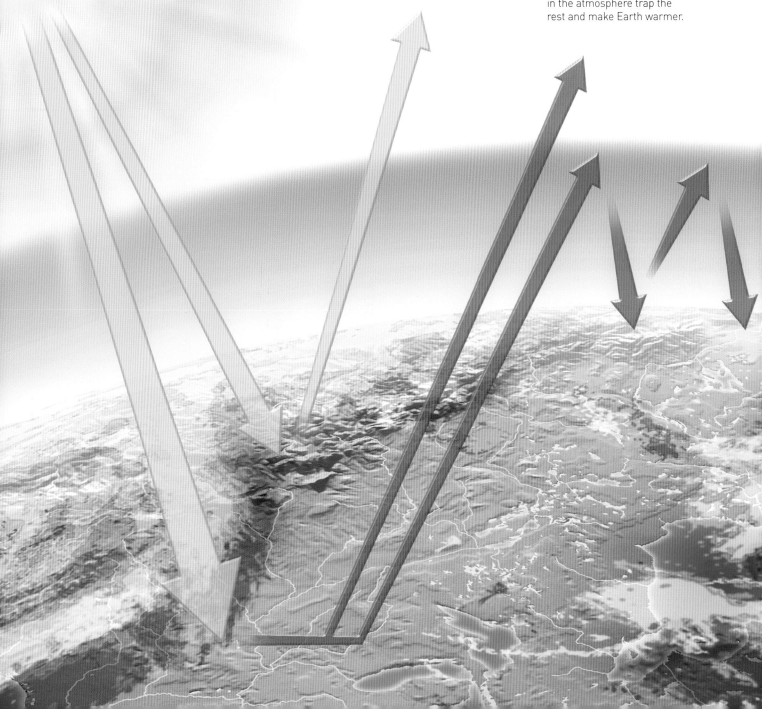

More people

The increasing number of people on Earth is one of the greatest factors in global warming. The world's population grew nearly four times larger during the past 100 years. More people means that more fossil fuels are burned. This has led to a massive rise in the levels of greenhouse gases in Earth's atmosphere.

Russia Russia is the most populated country in Europe. Moscow, its capital, is Europe's largest city.

Bangladesh A traffic jam clogs the streets of Dhaka in Bangladesh—the seventh most populated country on Earth.

United States A thick cloud of smog hangs over Los Angeles, California, where the population is almost 4 million.

China More than 100,000 babies are born in Beijing, China, every year. The population of China is about 1.3 billion people, more than four times greater than the United States.

Brazil More than 6 million people live Rio de Janeiro. Almost a million of them live in slums.

Swelling numbers

The world's population is growing by 80 million people a year, but it is not spread out evenly. Most growth is happening in cities—especially in Asia.

New York The United States has far fewer people than either China or India, but produces more greenhouse gases than any other country on Earth. This is because people in developed countries, such as the United States, use much more energy than those in less developed countries, such as China or India.

The largest populations

Each figure represents 100 million people.

China	1,313,974,000
India	1,111,714,000
United States	302,473,000
Indonesia	213,820,000
Brazil	188,078,000
Pakistan	161,744,000
Bangladesh	147,365,000
Russia	142,069,000
Nigeria	131,860,000
Japan	127,515,000
Mexico	107,450,000
Philippines	89,469,000

While you were reading this sentence, about 17 babies were born around the world.

Past, present, and future
In the past 200 years, the world's population rocketed from around a billion to more than 6.7 billion. By 2050, it is predicted that there will be more than 9 billion people on Earth, mostly living in Asia and Africa.

World population

8 billion
7 billion
6 billion
5 billion
4 billion
3 billion
2 billion
1 billion

Asia

Africa

Europe

Oceania

Latin America and the Caribbean

North America

Year   1600   1650   1700   1750   1800   1850   1900   1950   2000   2050

City life

It is not just that there are more people than ever before, it is also how we choose to live that puts a strain on our planet. Life in large cities is comfortable and convenient, but the energy this lifestyle requires has a high environmental cost.

Big burner The energy for most cities comes from power stations that burn fossil fuels to make electricity.

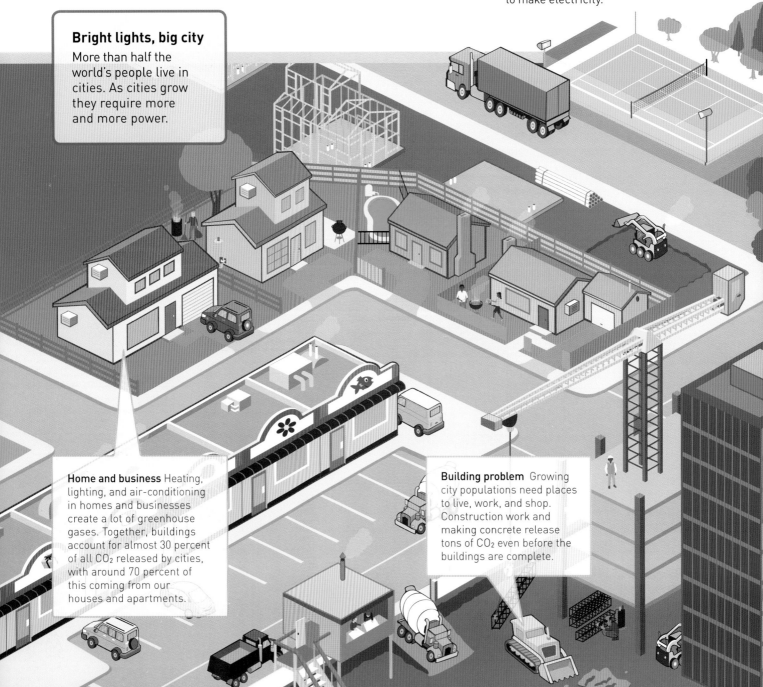

Bright lights, big city
More than half the world's people live in cities. As cities grow they require more and more power.

Home and business Heating, lighting, and air-conditioning in homes and businesses create a lot of greenhouse gases. Together, buildings account for almost 30 percent of all CO_2 released by cities, with around 70 percent of this coming from our houses and apartments.

Building problem Growing city populations need places to live, work, and shop. Construction work and making concrete release tons of CO_2 even before the buildings are complete.

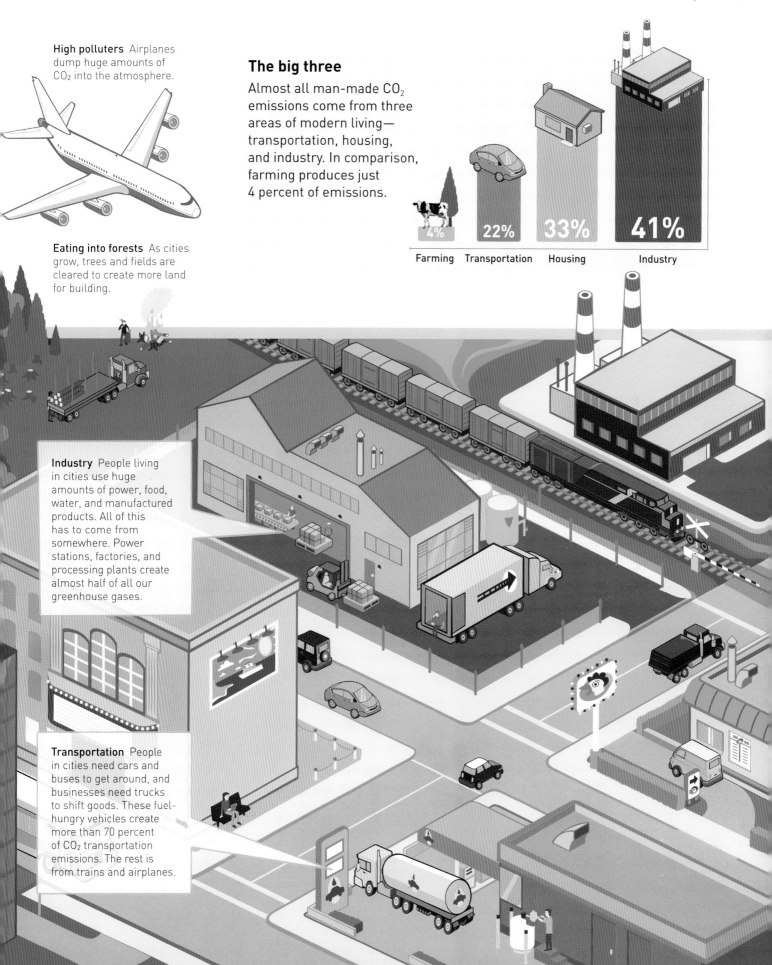

High polluters Airplanes dump huge amounts of CO$_2$ into the atmosphere.

Eating into forests As cities grow, trees and fields are cleared to create more land for building.

The big three

Almost all man-made CO$_2$ emissions come from three areas of modern living—transportation, housing, and industry. In comparison, farming produces just 4 percent of emissions.

4% Farming
22% Transportation
33% Housing
41% Industry

Industry People living in cities use huge amounts of power, food, water, and manufactured products. All of this has to come from somewhere. Power stations, factories, and processing plants create almost half of all our greenhouse gases.

Transportation People in cities need cars and buses to get around, and businesses need trucks to shift goods. These fuel-hungry vehicles create more than 70 percent of CO$_2$ transportation emissions. The rest is from trains and airplanes.

Disappearing ice A polar bear mother and her cubs walk across the ice near Churchill, Canada. Shrinking summer sea ice is a serious threat to the long-term survival of polar bears.

What does it mean for us?

Melting ice

2002

Melting ice is perhaps the most obvious effect of global warming. The vast ice sheets of the Arctic are getting smaller every year. Many glaciers—the huge rivers of ice that flow in slow motion down mountains—are disappearing completely. Melting ice contributes to rising sea levels, which could flood land and destroy homes in low-lying areas.

Going, going . . . Glaciers around the world are shrinking as temperatures rise and snowfalls change. Pictured right is Triftgletscher Glacier in Switzerland, one of many European glaciers that are disappearing.

Shrinking icebergs Ice at the North and South poles is shrinking, with some glaciers breaking off to form icebergs. Arctic sea ice, which gets larger in winter and smaller in summer, is expected to disappear completely every summer from 2030 onward.

2003

Ice reflector

As sea ice melts, there is less area of shiny surface to bounce back the Sun's energy. The sea around it absorbs more heat, causing the temperature of the sea to rise. This speeds up how fast the sea ice melts.

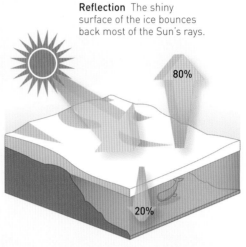

Reflection The shiny surface of the ice bounces back most of the Sun's rays.

80%

20%

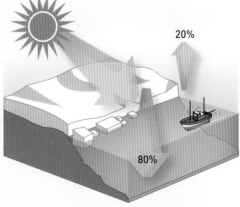

Faster As the ice melts, more of the Sun's rays are absorbed by the water. The water gets warmer and the ice melts faster.

20%

80%

90%
of all the ice
on Earth is in the
Antarctic ice sheet.

Sea levels have already risen by 8 inches (200 mm) over the last 100 years. That might not sound like much, but as the oceans warm and glaciers melt, levels will continue to rise faster and faster. Before too long, many low-lying villages, towns, cities, and islands will be threatened by flooding.

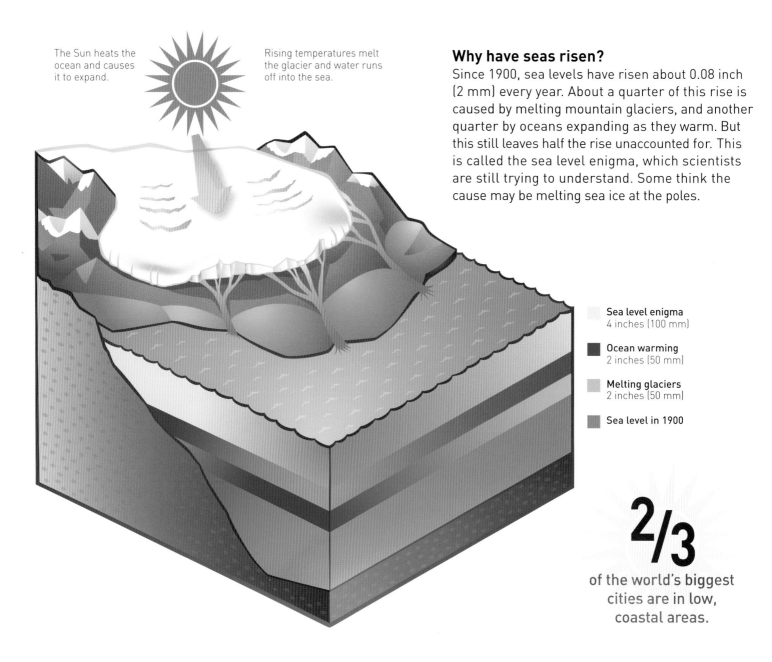

The Sun heats the ocean and causes it to expand.

Rising temperatures melt the glacier and water runs off into the sea.

Why have seas risen?

Since 1900, sea levels have risen about 0.08 inch (2 mm) every year. About a quarter of this rise is caused by melting mountain glaciers, and another quarter by oceans expanding as they warm. But this still leaves half the rise unaccounted for. This is called the sea level enigma, which scientists are still trying to understand. Some think the cause may be melting sea ice at the poles.

Sea level enigma
4 inches (100 mm)

Ocean warming
2 inches (50 mm)

Melting glaciers
2 inches (50 mm)

Sea level in 1900

2/3
of the world's biggest cities are in low, coastal areas.

Deep trouble The tiny islands of Tuvalu, right, are about halfway between Hawaii and Australia. Rising seas have already flooded many areas. People who live on these islands may eventually have to abandon them and move to higher land.

Shishmaref The residents of the coastal town of Shishmaref, Alaska, have already felt the effect of rising sea levels due to global warming. Increasingly high tides are washing away the foundations of their houses, which then collapse.

How far will sea levels rise?

If sea levels continue rising at their current rate, they will be around 19 inches (480 mm) higher by 2100, shown here as an orange line. But this is not certain, and additional warming and ice melting in Greenland or Antarctica could push this level up to 39 inches (1,000 mm) or higher (green line).

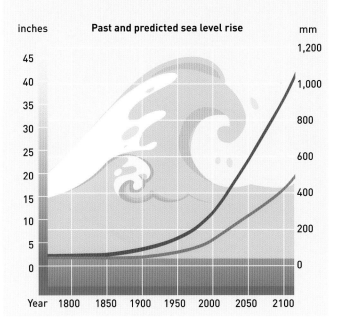

inches **Past and predicted sea level rise** mm

inches		mm
45		1,200
40		1,000
35		
30		800
25		600
20		
15		400
10		200
5		
0		0

Year 1800 1850 1900 1950 2000 2050 2100

Wetter, drier

Changes in weather patterns can cause both heavy rains and severe drought. We are already experiencing the effects of changing rainfall as it increases in some regions and decreases in others. Some scientists predict that global warming will make many wet regions even wetter and dry regions even drier. And as sea temperatures rise, existing climate problems such as drought, desertification, and flooding may become more common and more destructive.

2002

Dry down under Record high temperatures hit Australia in 2002, causing one of the most widespread droughts in its history. About 60 percent of the country had little rain for nine months of the year. The drying of Lake Burrendong in New South Wales (above and right) caused severe water shortages in nearby towns.

Effects of desertification

Desertification happens when desert sands slowly shift to cover neighboring areas. This can destroy fields and ruin villages. It is caused largely by changes in wind patterns. Droughts linked to climate change may make the problem worse in some areas.

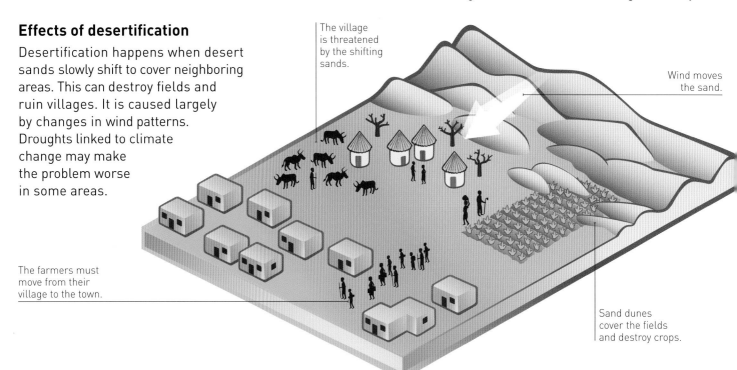

The village is threatened by the shifting sands.

Wind moves the sand.

The farmers must move from their village to the town.

Sand dunes cover the fields and destroy crops.

2003

Water wars

Lake Chad was once one of Africa's largest lakes, but after 30 years of drought it has shrunk to 5 percent of its former size. This has caused fights between farmers in the region who depend on it for water.

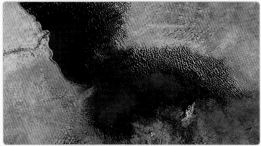

Lake Chad in 1973

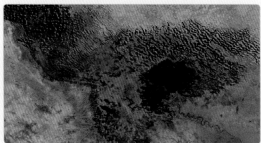

Lake Chad in 2001

Changing rainfall

Global warming does not affect the total amount of rain that falls on Earth, but it can have a big effect on local climates by exaggerating changes to rainfall caused by other weather patterns.

This map shows the change in rainfall across the planet since 1900. The larger the sun, the bigger the decrease in rainfall. The larger the rain drop, the bigger the increase in rainfall.

-50%   -40%   -30%   -20%   -10%   0%   +10%   +20%   +30%   +40%   +50%

Extreme weather

Many scientists believe that we can already see signs of climate change in the form of extreme weather around the world. Hurricanes, forest fires, and other weather-related disasters have always occurred, but some seem to be getting stronger and more frequent as the world's atmosphere and oceans get warmer.

Hurricanes

Hurricanes, also called cyclones and typhoons, form over tropical oceans, where they are powered by warm surface waters. As seas get warmer, these monster storms are expected to become even stronger.

Floods Heavy rains, rising seas, and large, surging waves can flood homes and threaten the lives of people and animals.

Wildfires As temperatures rise, forests and farms can dry out and catch fire to create massive wildfires. Left unchecked, these fires can burn vast areas of precious forest and destroy homes.

Heat waves Prolonged hot weather can be deadly, especially for young children and old people. The number and length of heat waves are expected to rise because of global warming.

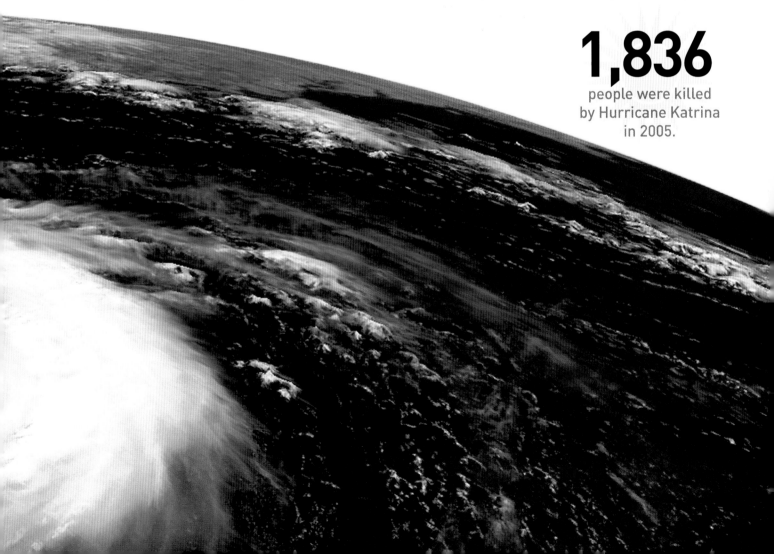

1,836
people were killed by Hurricane Katrina in 2005.

Pollution problems

Burning fossil fuels, the major cause of global warming, also causes air pollution. Exhaust gases from factories, cars, and other vehicles contain greenhouse gases that trap heat in our atmosphere. As well as making Earth warmer, some of these gases can create smog and acid rain.

Smog masks A traffic officer, in Kolkata, India, wears a face mask to protect himself from air pollution. Smog causes more than 1.6 million deaths worldwide each year

How smog is created

Smog is formed when exhaust gases from cars and factories react with oxygen in the air, warmed by high temperatures and ultraviolet rays from the Sun. This creates a thick cloud of nitrogen dioxide, ozone, and other harmful gases, which can irritate or even permanently damage the lungs.

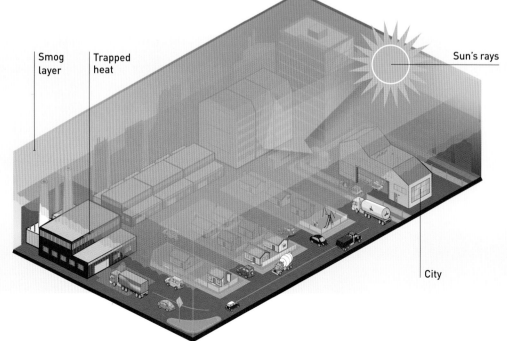

Smog layer

Trapped heat

Sun's rays

City

Mexico City Less than 30 years ago, Mexico City was considered one of the cleanest cities in the world. It is now one of the most polluted. A thick layer of smog covers the city, and the volcanoes that dot the horizon can no longer be seen.

Children are three times more likely to develop asthma if they live in a smoggy area.

Heat island effect

Concrete buildings and sidewalks trap heat during the day, leaving cities and towns several degrees warmer than surrounding country areas in the evenings. This is called the heat island effect. The increased heat in cities and towns also leads to higher levels of air pollution.

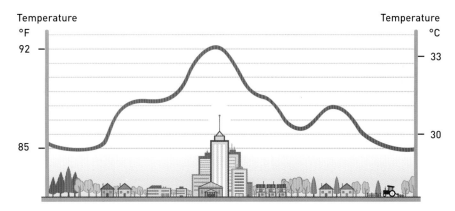

Temperature °F
92
85

Temperature °C
33
30

More disease

A rise in temperature around the world is expected to cause an increase in infectious diseases. Flooding could transmit diseases, such as typhoid and cholera, that spread in water. Also, the number of insects that carry diseases may increase, move to warmer areas, and spread sicknesses, such as malaria and encephalitis, to new places.

Fever on the rise

As temperatures rise, so does the number of people who get infectious diseases. For example, if the temperature of San Diego, California, rises by 3.6°F (2°C), the number of cases of dengue fever will almost double. A rise of 5.4°F (3°C) will see the number of cases triple.

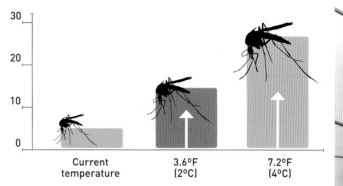

Cases of dengue fever
in San Diego, California

Current temperature	3.6°F (2°C)	7.2°F (4°C)

Disease reaching out

Malaria is already found in more than 100 countries. As temperatures rise, the mosquitoes that carry malaria may spread to new regions, such as Scandinavia and the UK, which are currently too cold to support them.

What can be done? A young child is weighed before receiving an injection, as part of a malaria vaccine trial in Manhica, Mozambique. More than 900,000 Africans die from malaria each year. Most of these are children.

Ticks Ticks can carry the deadly brain disease encephalitis. In northern Europe the number of cases is growing, and scientists have linked the increase to unusually warm winters.

Disease carriers Some kinds of mosquitoes carry germs in their saliva, which they transfer to humans when they bite. The germs then travel through the person's blood to the liver, causing malaria, which can be deadly if not treated.

The enemy within Malaria is caused by the plasmodium parasite—a very small creature that lives inside liver and blood cells.

Disappearing world

Over the course of Earth's history, plant and animal species have naturally died out. But we are now losing species at between 100 and 1,000 times the natural rate, and almost all of this increase is caused by humans. While hunting and habitat destruction play a major part, climate change and the problems it causes, such as higher temperatures, changing rainfall, and extreme weather, make the situation more serious.

More than 16,000 plant and animal species are now threatened with extinction.

Pacific hawksbill turtle

Pacific hawksbill turtles live in the Caribbean, where six out of seven turtle species are now endangered. Global warming affects turtles a great deal, for a number of reasons:

- Sea grasses and corals, which turtles feed on, are dying in warmer oceans.

- Remote island beaches where turtles nest are disappearing as sea levels rise.

- Turtles struggle to find nesting beaches because of shifting ocean currents.

- When temperatures are higher, turtle eggs fail to hatch or all hatch as females, which means there are fewer chances to breed.

Apollo butterfly This butterfly lives in mountain meadows and needs sunlight to stay warm and survive. But a warming climate has enabled trees to grow higher up mountains, blocking out their precious sunlight.

Trout Fish that were once common in cold water are becoming rare in many areas, as freshwater lakes and rivers warm up. Trout and salmon are especially sensitive to temperature change

Shrinking ice Polar bears hunt from the ice. As temperatures rise and the ice disappears, polar bears have less opportunity to feed. This means a shorter lifespan and fewer cubs.

Numbers game

The World Conservation Union gathers information from scientists every few years to estimate the number of threatened species. Recent studies show that in almost all animal groups, more and more species are becoming threatened each year. As many as 1 in 3 amphibians and 1 in 4 mammals are currently under threat.

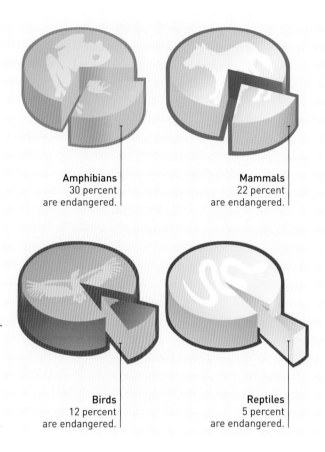

Amphibians
30 percent
are endangered.

Mammals
22 percent
are endangered.

Birds
12 percent
are endangered.

Reptiles
5 percent
are endangered.

Golden toad This rare toad became extinct in 1987. It was killed by a disease that spread quickly through its forest habitat because of unusually warm temperatures.

Curlew The curlew, like many other shorebirds worldwide, is becoming increasingly threatened as its habitat, food supplies, and migration patterns are changed by global warming.

Pika This small relative of rabbits is heading for extinction, unable to survive the warming of its mountain habitat. It could become the first mammal to die because of climate change.

Clean energy Solar energy is the most abundant source of energy on Earth. One of the important technological challenges we face is how to harvest solar energy cheaply and efficiently.

What are we doing?

Working together

For a huge problem like climate change, we need big, global solutions. That means the whole world working together, with scientists gathering and sharing information, and governments taking action to find solutions. International efforts, such as the Kyoto Protocol, are a good start, but there is still much more to be done.

The journey to Kyoto

The Kyoto Protocol brought more than 170 countries together with the common goal of battling climate change. But it did not happen overnight. It took almost 18 years to create the plan.

1987	United Nations (UN) countries work together to ban CFCs.
1988	UN forms the Intergovernmental Panel on Climate Change (IPCC) to gather and present information from scientists working on climate change.
1992	The IPCC makes its first report.
1992	UN Framework Convention on Climate Change is produced, and signed by 166 countries. The UN asks countries to assess their own greenhouse emissions, and agree to do something about them.
1997	UN meets in Kyoto, Japan, and makes plans for serious changes to greenhouse emissions—the Kyoto Protocol.
2005	The Kyoto Protocol is signed by 141 countries.

Progress so far

In 1992, more than 160 countries agreed that by the year 2000 they would cut their greenhouse gas emissions down to the levels they were at in 1990. This chart shows changes in emissions from 1990 to 2003. Orange lines show increases in emissions; green lines show decreases.

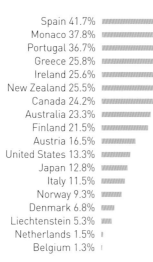

Spain 41.7%
Monaco 37.8%
Portugal 36.7%
Greece 25.8%
Ireland 25.6%
New Zealand 25.5%
Canada 24.2%
Australia 23.3%
Finland 21.5%
Austria 16.5%
United States 13.3%
Japan 12.8%
Italy 11.5%
Norway 9.3%
Denmark 6.8%
Liechtenstein 5.3%
Netherlands 1.5%
Belgium 1.3%

Big Difference While Lithuania and Latvia decreased their emissions by around 60 percent, countries such as Spain and Portugal increased emissions by about 40 percent over the same period.

Switzerland 0.4%
European community 1%
Slovenia 1.8%
France 1.9%
Sweden 2.3%
Croatia 6%
Iceland 8.2%
United Kingdom 13%
Luxembourg 16.1%
Germany 18.2%
Czech Republic 28.3%
Slovakia 28.3%
Hungary 31.9%
Poland 34.4%
Russian Federation 38%
Belarus 50.5%
Estonia 50.8%
Latvia 58.8%
Lithuania 66.2%

Russia signs up Activists gathered outside the Russian parliament in April 2004, as politicians inside discussed whether to sign the Kyoto Protocol. The government agreed to do so on November 18, 2004.

Council effort The city council of Barcelona, Spain, hopes to distribute 3,000 of these special bikes. They can be borrowed for free, and are a clean alternative to driving a car, which releases greenhouse gases.

Rule makers Despite the success of the Kyoto Protocol, there is still work to be done. Australia, Turkey, and the United States have not yet signed the Kyoto Protocol. Talks, such as this one in Germany, are still going on to find the best way to slow global warming.

CFC victory

The Kyoto Protocol followed an earlier international success. With the Montreal Protocol in 1987, 189 countries banned the use of CFC chemicals that destroy ozone. Although the seasonal hole in the ozone layer over Antarctica is still growing, it is now growing at a much slower rate.

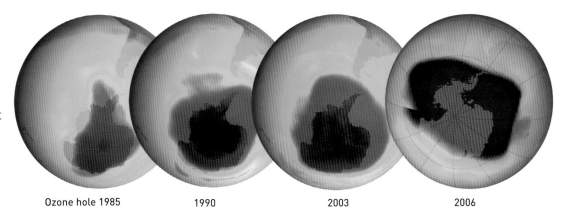

Ozone hole 1985   1990   2003   2006

Cleaner energy

If we want to stop climate change, rather than just slow it down, we need to do more than just reduce the amount of fossil fuels we burn. We must switch to alternative energies, ideally from sources that produce low amounts of greenhouse gas and that are renewable. Our supply of fossil fuels will one day be completely used up, but renewable energies are unlimited. They rely on sunlight and Earth's natural cycles and will never run out.

Push and pull Tidal turbines work like wind turbines placed underwater. The push and pull of tidal currents turns the rotors and generates electricity.

Renewables on the rise

Renewable power sources include wind, solar, wave, tidal, hydroelectric, and biomass energies. Fifteen percent of the world's electricity comes from hydroelectric power, which is created when a rush of dam water spins turbines that generate electricity. Other renewable power sources are used far less, but are becoming more popular.

Wind power Wind turbines work in a similar way to windmills. Wind turns the rotors, but instead of driving a millstone as in a windmill, the rotors in a wind turbine drive a generator that creates electricity. The largest turbines can generate enough energy to power a small town.

A special power station in the UK runs completely on bird droppings.

Solar farm This solar power plant in the United States is one of many around the world that makes electricity without releasing any greenhouse gas. The mirrors concentrate the Sun's energy at a focal point on top of the tower, creating heat that is used to drive a series of turbines.

Solar cell

Solar cells use silicon crystals to convert sunlight into electricity. As light strikes the crystals, electric charges are knocked loose and channeled into wires.

Nuclear power plant Some scientists recommend using nuclear power, rather than fossil fuels, until renewable energy sources are better developed. But while nuclear fuels produce less greenhouse gas than fossil fuels, they create dangerous radioactive wastes.

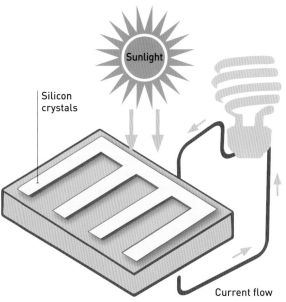

Sunlight

Silicon crystals

Current flow

Cleaner transportation

The exhaust gases from vehicles account for about a quarter of all the carbon dioxide we release. As more people buy cars and take cheap flights, transportation emissions are increasing. But by designing more efficient cars, buses, and airplanes, and moving toward new kinds of fuel, engineers are helping to clean up the future of travel.

Car of the future

Hybrid cars release fewer greenhouse gases than regular cars. This is because some of the time they are powered partly or completely by electricity that the car itself has generated.

Biofuels Though most hybrid cars run on regular unleaded gasoline, drivers in some countries use cleaner alternatives. Biofuels, such as ethanol and biodiesel, are made from plant oils rather than fossil fuels. The amount of carbon that biofuels release when they are burned is much less than regular gasoline.

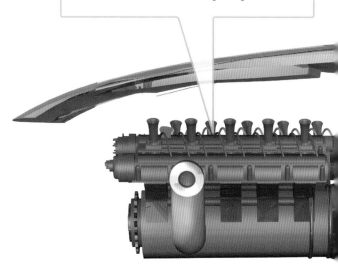

Green bus This bus runs on hydrogen instead of gasoline or diesel. Unlike a regular bus, it does not release any greenhouse gas. Iceland was the first country to test hydrogen-powered city buses.

Wonder fuel Hydrogen buses are filled up at special hydrogen fueling stations. The hydrogen is converted directly into electricity and the only exhaust gas is pure water vapor.

The number of cars in the world is expected to double over the next 30 years.

Modes of transportation

Different forms of transportation produce different amounts of CO_2 per person per mile. Cars are the most popular, yet the least efficient way to travel. Although buses and airplanes use more fuel than cars, they can carry many people at once, which means they release less carbon per passenger. Almost no CO_2 is released by cycling or walking.

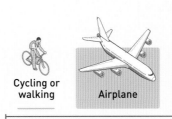

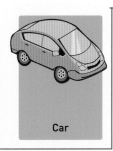

Cycling or walking	Airplane	Public transportation	Car
0	0.44 pound per passenger, per mile (0.20 kg/km)	0.70 pound per passenger, per mile (0.30 kg/km)	1 pound per passenger, per mile (0.45 kg/km)

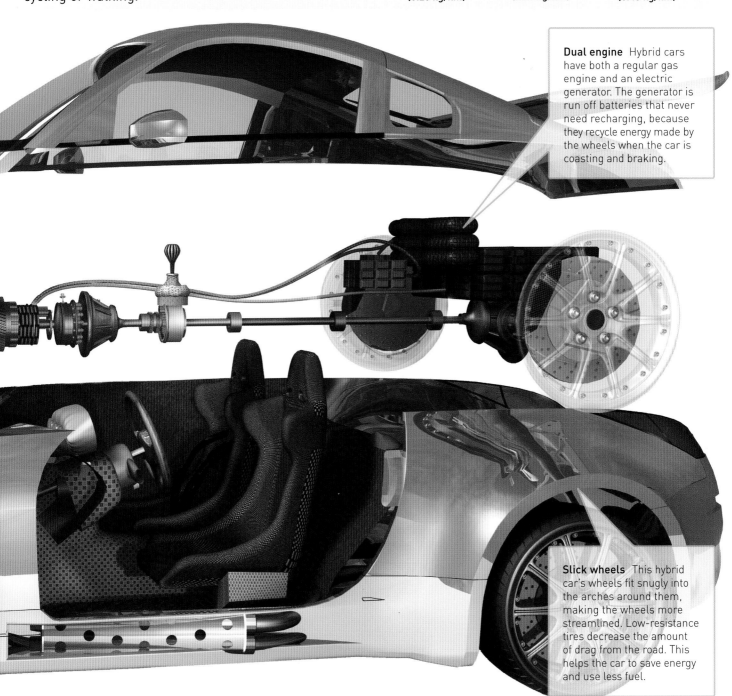

Dual engine Hybrid cars have both a regular gas engine and an electric generator. The generator is run off batteries that never need recharging, because they recycle energy made by the wheels when the car is coasting and braking.

Slick wheels This hybrid car's wheels fit snugly into the arches around them, making the wheels more streamlined. Low-resistance tires decrease the amount of drag from the road. This helps the car to save energy and use less fuel.

Eco homes

Almost a third of the greenhouse gas we produce comes from our homes. The good news is that there are many ways, ranging from how our homes are built to the way we live inside them, by which we can reduce the amount of greenhouse gas we create.

Be eco-friendly in your own home

This eco-friendly house has many features that save energy. If everyone used just one or two of these in their own home, we could reduce the amount of greenhouse gas that our houses release into the atmosphere.

Greenroof This house in Frankfurt, Germany, has a sloping roof covered with a "skin," on which grass is planted. The greenroof helps keep the house warm in winter and cool in summer without using as much energy as a regular house.

Recycling bins Separate bins for recycling ensure that the maximum amount of household waste is recycled, instead of ending up in landfill.

Composting Food scraps from the kitchen and grass clippings from the lawn are composted to reduce waste and provide fertilizer for the garden.

Greenhouse Sunlight hitting the greenhouse is used to heat water for the under-floor system. Hot air in the greenhouse can also be channeled into the house to heat rooms.

Living room The walls, windows, and ceilings of the living room are insulated. Light comes from reflective skylights, or sun tubes, which collect sunlight at roof level and direct it to the room below.

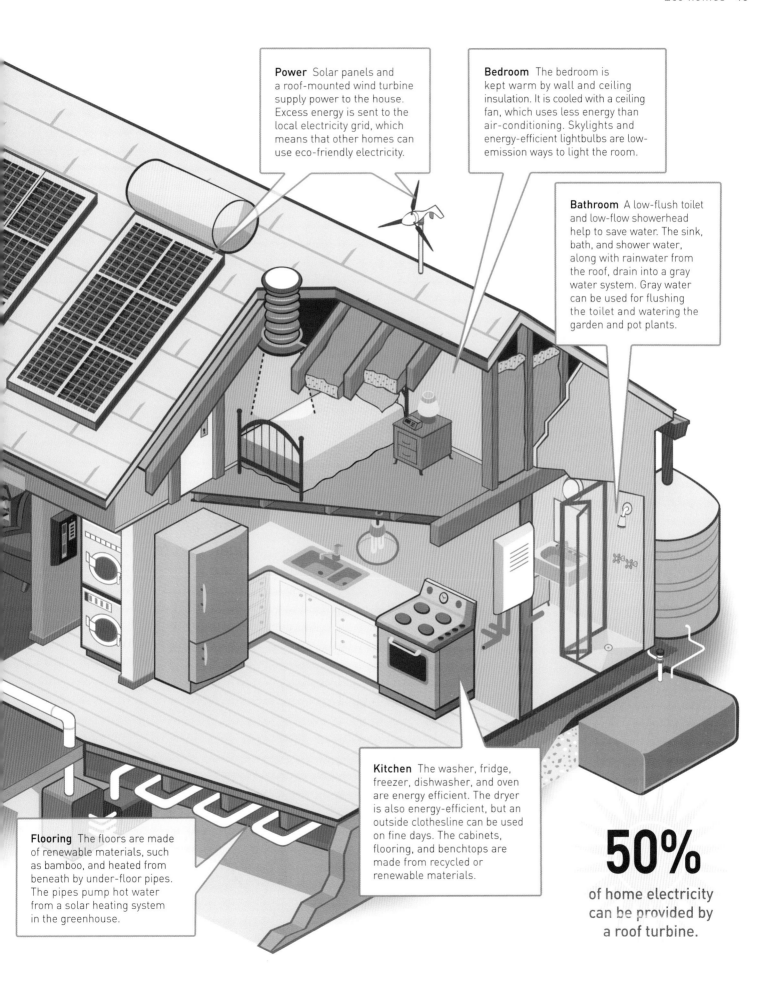

Power Solar panels and a roof-mounted wind turbine supply power to the house. Excess energy is sent to the local electricity grid, which means that other homes can use eco-friendly electricity.

Bedroom The bedroom is kept warm by wall and ceiling insulation. It is cooled with a ceiling fan, which uses less energy than air-conditioning. Skylights and energy-efficient lightbulbs are low-emission ways to light the room.

Bathroom A low-flush toilet and low-flow showerhead help to save water. The sink, bath, and shower water, along with rainwater from the roof, drain into a gray water system. Gray water can be used for flushing the toilet and watering the garden and pot plants.

Kitchen The washer, fridge, freezer, dishwasher, and oven are energy efficient. The dryer is also energy-efficient, but an outside clothesline can be used on fine days. The cabinets, flooring, and benchtops are made from recycled or renewable materials.

Flooring The floors are made of renewable materials, such as bamboo, and heated from beneath by under-floor pipes. The pipes pump hot water from a solar heating system in the greenhouse.

50%
of home electricity can be provided by a roof turbine.

Preserving forests and oceans

Forests and oceans remove and trap carbon as part of their natural processes. In turn, they can reduce the amount of carbon dioxide in the atmosphere and limit the power of the greenhouse effect. By damaging forests, polluting oceans, and burning fossil fuels, humans have upset Earth's natural balance. This is why we must work together to protect our precious trees and seas.

Reforestation Tree-planting projects like the United Nations Billion Tree Campaign are global initiatives that aim to replace lost forests by planting new ones.

State of the world's forests

The world's forests are not spread evenly across the globe. Most are found in the Northern Hemisphere—in Russia and North America—where they are gradually being eaten away by logging. Rain forests cover parts of South America and Southeast Asia, where trees are burned to create farmland.

In the last 40 years more than half of our planet's original forests have been lost.

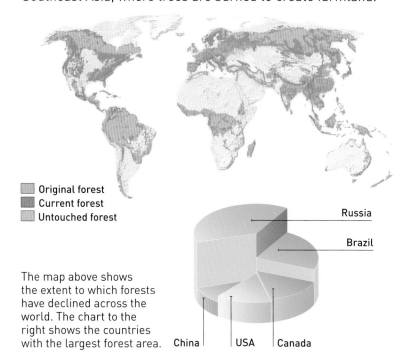

Original forest
Current forest
Untouched forest

Russia

Brazil

The map above shows the extent to which forests have declined across the world. The chart to the right shows the countries with the largest forest area.

China   USA   Canada

Brazil The rain forest in Brazil is being destroyed to make room for cattle ranches and farms. Since 2000, an area larger than Greece has been cleared.

Studying sea life Scientists are carefully monitoring the effects of global warming on sea life. Some countries have created marine reserves to protect threatened species.

Phytoplankton Phytoplankton are tiny ocean plants that remove more carbon dioxide from the atmosphere than all other trees and plants put together. But as carbon builds up in the oceans, the seawater may become too acidic for phytoplankton to survive.

Keeping the balance

Forests and oceans help to control carbon dioxide levels in the atmosphere by storing carbon. This is why they are sometimes called carbon sinks. Together, forests and oceans provide a balance to the natural and man-made sources that release greenhouse gases.

Forests Forests remove large amounts of carbon from the atmosphere as they grow. They release some carbon dioxide during their lifecycle, and as they decompose. But they remove more than they release.

Oceans Some of the carbon in the atmosphere dissolves into oceans. Marine plants, such as phytoplankton and algae, absorb some of the carbon and trap it in their bodies. The rest is recycled back into the atmosphere.

Changing land use When we change the function of land, by cutting down forests to create farmland for example, we release more carbon into the atmosphere than the planted crops are able to absorb.

Humans Factories, vehicles, and power stations burn fuels formed by fossilized plant and animal remains, releasing huge amounts of trapped carbon into the atmosphere in an instant. This artificial release is not balanced by any natural trapping process.

You can make a difference Taking care of Earth is everyone's responsibility. It only takes a little effort to make a big difference in the place where you live.

What can you do?

Measure your carbon footprint

A carbon footprint is an estimate of how much carbon dioxide is released into the atmosphere as a result of someone's actions. By measuring the size of your footprint, and taking steps to reduce it, you and your family can start the battle against global warming at home. If you support programs that decrease, or offset, carbon usage, you might even reduce your carbon footprint to zero.

Today, the average person uses more than four times as much energy as a person 100 years ago.

Carbon offsets

Reducing your carbon footprint can be difficult, especially if your area does not use renewable energy, or if you have to travel to work or school. The good news is that you can make up for the greenhouse gases your actions cause by supporting offset programs that remove carbon from the atmosphere.

Biofuels Biofuel programs work to make alternatives to fossil fuels from plant and animal sources—like corn, sugar cane, and even pig manure.

Green bulbs Low-energy lightbulb programs distribute energy-efficient lightbulbs in developing countries. These replace the less efficient, traditional bulbs many people use.

Trees Reforestation programs support the planting of new trees, to replace those lost to logging and burning.

Energy Renewable energy programs support the building of environmentally friendly energy sources, such as windfarms, which help cut fossil fuel usage.

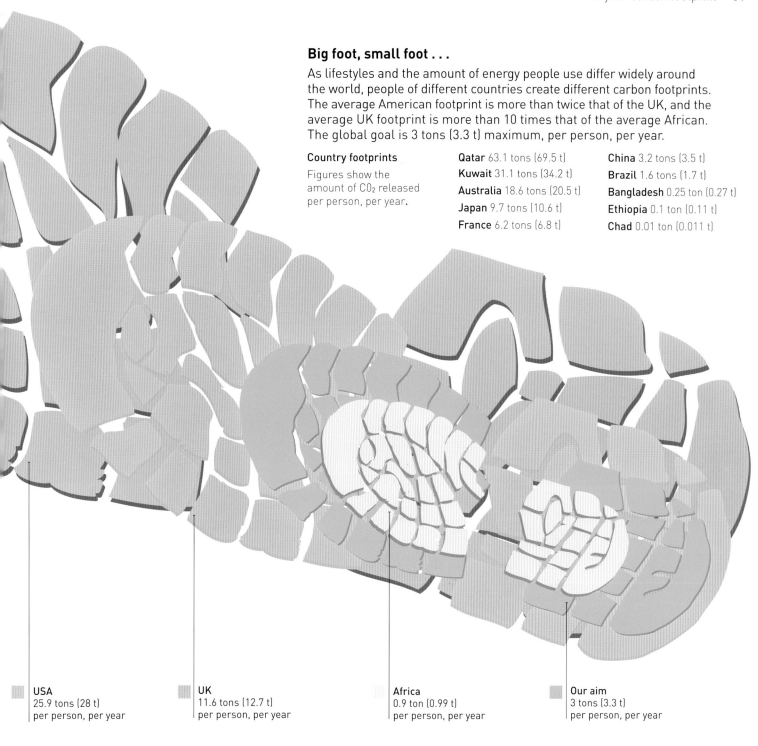

Big foot, small foot . . .

As lifestyles and the amount of energy people use differ widely around the world, people of different countries create different carbon footprints. The average American footprint is more than twice that of the UK, and the average UK footprint is more than 10 times that of the average African. The global goal is 3 tons (3.3 t) maximum, per person, per year.

Country footprints

Figures show the amount of CO_2 released per person, per year.

Qatar 63.1 tons (69.5 t)
Kuwait 31.1 tons (34.2 t)
Australia 18.6 tons (20.5 t)
Japan 9.7 tons (10.6 t)
France 6.2 tons (6.8 t)

China 3.2 tons (3.5 t)
Brazil 1.6 tons (1.7 t)
Bangladesh 0.25 ton (0.27 t)
Ethiopia 0.1 ton (0.11 t)
Chad 0.01 ton (0.011 t)

USA
25.9 tons (28 t)
per person, per year

UK
11.6 tons (12.7 t)
per person, per year

Africa
0.9 ton (0.99 t)
per person, per year

Our aim
3 tons (3.3 t)
per person, per year

what can you do?

Calculate your carbon footprint

Calculating your own carbon footprint can be tricky, but there are many free online carbon calculators available to help you do it. Check out one of the websites listed below, and ask your family for help with gathering the information needed.

• www.resurgence.org/carboncalculator/
• www.earthlab.com
• www.myfootprint.org
• www.bp.com/carbonfootprint

**6 tons
(6.6 t)**

is the current world average for carbon dioxide released per person, per year.

Save energy

One easy way to shrink your carbon footprint is to conserve energy. Most of us waste energy when heating, cooling, and lighting our homes, and when running electrical appliances and gadgets. Small steps like changing lightbulbs and switching off gadgets might not seem important, but they can help to reduce greenhouse gas emissions.

Televisions on "standby" can use over half the energy they do when switched on.

300

pounds (135 kg) of CO_2 gas are saved each year by every CFL bulb.

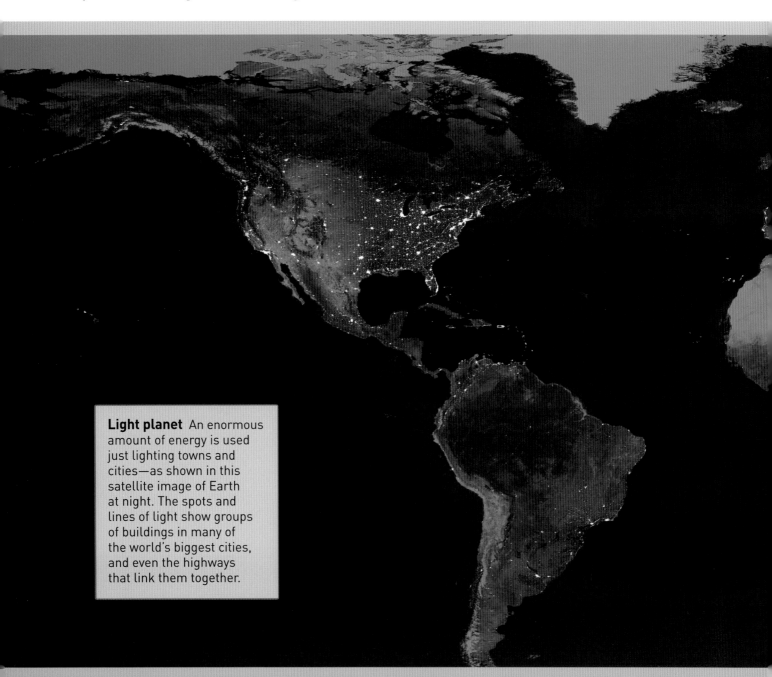

Light planet An enormous amount of energy is used just lighting towns and cities—as shown in this satellite image of Earth at night. The spots and lines of light show groups of buildings in many of the world's biggest cities, and even the highways that link them together.

what can you do ?

1 **Replace every traditional lightbulb** in the house with an energy-efficient CFL bulb.

2 **Turn televisions**, computers, and other electronics to "off," instead of "standby" or "sleep."

3 **Always unplug chargers** for cell phones and mp3 players after use.

4 **Turn down central heating** in winter, and wear a sweater to keep warm.

5 **Turn down air-conditioning** in summer, or turn it off and use a fan instead.

Better lightbulbs

Compact Fluorescent Lamps (CFLs) give out the same amount of light as traditional lightbulbs, but they use around 75 percent less energy and last 10 times longer. If every house in the United States replaced just one bulb, the CO_2 gas saved would be the same as taking 1.3 million cars off the road.

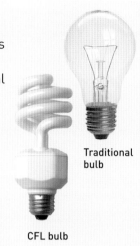

Traditional bulb

CFL bulb

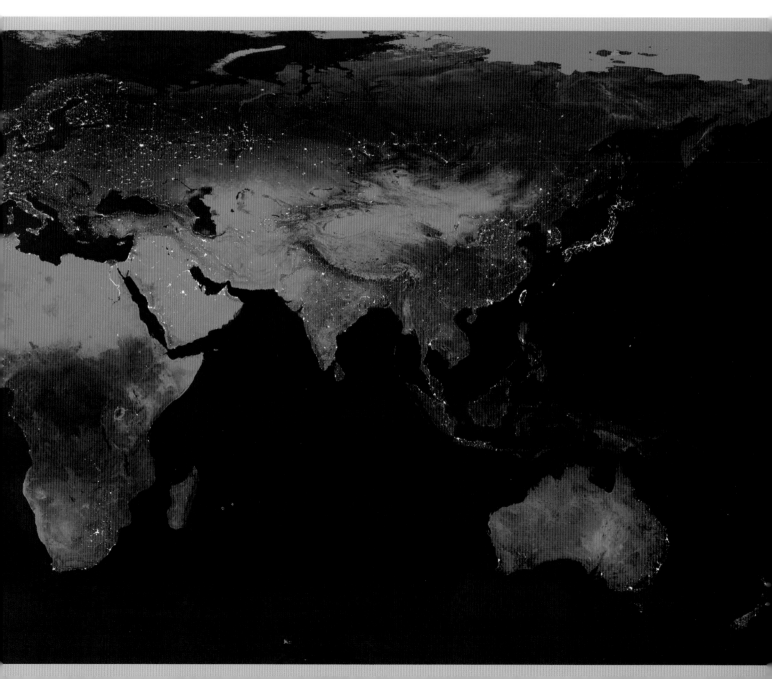

Water world

The amount of fresh water available is different for different countries. Also, each country uses different amounts of water for drinking, washing, and watering crops. As climate and weather patterns change, water could become hard to find in many places.

The colors on the map show the amount of fresh water that is available in selected countries.

- Extremely low
- Very low
- Low
- Average
- High
- Very high
- No information

The glasses show the amount of water used per person, per year, for selected countries.

United States
57,000 cubic feet
(1,600 m^3)

United Kingdom
7,000 cubic feet
(197 m^3)

Mexico
26,000 cubic feet
(731 m^3)

Brazil
11,000 cubic feet
(318 m^3)

1%
of water on Earth is fresh water.

Save water

Saving water also saves the energy used to collect, treat, and pump it. So not using as much water can help cut the amount of greenhouse gas released and fight global warming. Water use varies across the world, but we can all do our part to make sure we are not wasting water.

what can you do?

1 **Turn the faucet off** when brushing your teeth.

2 **Take quick showers** instead of long baths.

3 **Do not use dishwashers** too often—wash by hand.

4 **Use short toilet flushes** wherever possible.

5 **Collect rainwater** for watering your plants.

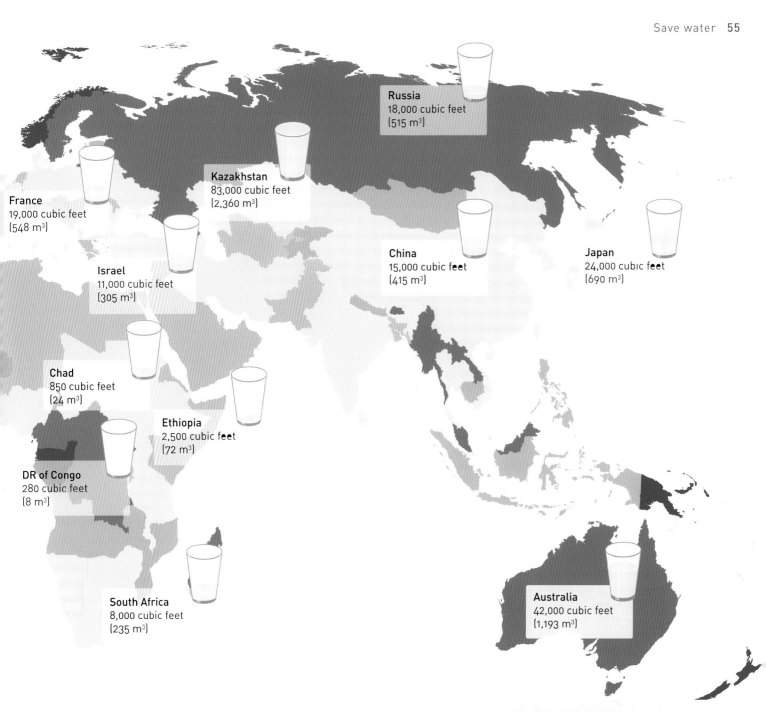

Russia
18,000 cubic feet
(515 m³)

Kazakhstan
83,000 cubic feet
(2,360 m³)

France
19,000 cubic feet
(548 m³)

China
15,000 cubic feet
(415 m³)

Japan
24,000 cubic feet
(690 m³)

Israel
11,000 cubic feet
(305 m³)

Chad
850 cubic feet
(24 m³)

Ethiopia
2,500 cubic feet
(72 m³)

DR of Congo
280 cubic feet
(8 m³)

South Africa
8,000 cubic feet
(235 m³)

Australia
42,000 cubic feet
(1,193 m³)

Household waste

Household appliances guzzle hundreds of gallons of water each month, so use them sparingly.

Washing machine
22 gallons
(83 l)
per load

Toilet
2 gallons
(8 l)
per flush

Dishwasher
11 gallons
(42 l)
per load

Bath
18 gallons
(68 l)
per bath

Water habits

Over the past 100 years, the world's increasing population has been using and wasting more water. Increasing amounts of water are lost to evaporation from the pipes, rivers, and dams supplying homes and businesses.

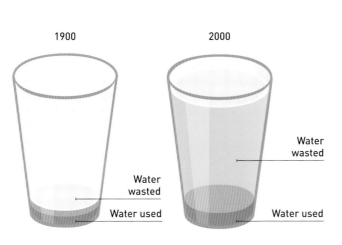

1900

2000

Water wasted

Water wasted

Water used

Water wasted

Water used

Less waste

Most of our household waste ends up in solid waste landfills. These huge trash dumps release methane—a greenhouse gas—as they rot. One simple way to cut the methane that is released is to reduce the amount of trash you produce, and recycle as much as possible of what is left.

Recycling plastic Workers in China sort different types of plastic before it is sent to be recycled. China imports huge amounts of plastic and paper that other countries have thrown out and turns them into new products.

What is in the trash can?

This chart shows how much of each type of waste is found in the typical landfill of a developed country. Composting and recycling can cut up to 90 percent of these waste products, saving energy and reducing greenhouse gases.

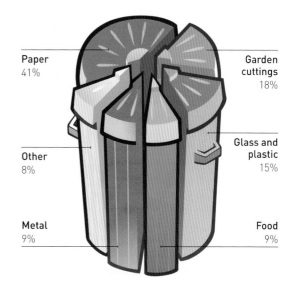

Paper 41%

Garden cuttings 18%

Other 8%

Glass and plastic 15%

Metal 9%

Food 9%

Garbage power

Special machines, called bioreactors, can use waste as a fuel to make electricity. Some places cleverly combine a landfill and power station into one. Methane is collected from buried waste and burned in a generator. This reduces the methane that is released and makes electricity.

Liquid The liquid from the rotting waste is circulated back into the waste to make it break down faster.

Generator The generator converts the methane into power.

Energy Power from the generator is sent to houses and businesses.

Buried waste Waste is buried under the ground, where it rots and gives off methane.

Methane The methane is collected in pipes and sent to the generator.

Recycle symbol The recycle symbol was designed in 1970 by an American college student as a label for recyclable containers. It is now recognized and used around the world for all kinds of recycling.

what can you do?

1 **Recycle as much waste** as is possible by sorting your trash.

2 **Compost all your food scraps** for use in your garden.

3 **Take used glass bottles** and jars to a recycling center.

4 **Save and reread old comics** and magazines, or give them to a friend.

5 **Donate old toys** and clothes to thrift stores.

One green day

Each one of us can help fight climate change by using less water and electricity. But if you really want to make a difference, you can go even further. The clothes you wear, the foods you eat, and the products you use all contribute to your personal carbon footprint. Simple, everyday decisions can make a huge difference to the amount of greenhouse gas that your lifestyle contributes to our atmosphere.

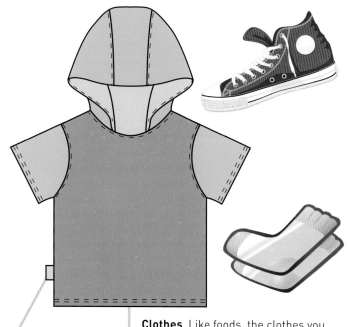

Clothes Like foods, the clothes you wear can clock up thousands of miles, and tons of carbon emissions, on their way to you, especially if they are made overseas. Buying locally made clothes can cut these emissions in half.

Label Have a look at the labels on your clothes to see where they were made.

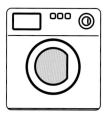

Wash time Wait for a full load before washing your clothes to save water.

Wake up Small, daily energy savings can make a big difference when multiplied over a lifetime. Digital alarm clocks use electricity all day long, while wind-up clocks use none at all, creating zero greenhouse gas.

What you can do in the morning

Shower Low-flow showerheads use less water and save on the energy needed to heat it. A low-flow showerhead can save around 350 pounds (158 kg) of carbon dioxide emissions per year. Showering for 6 minutes rather than 10 minutes saves even more water.

Breakfast Cereals, fruits, and meats travel an average of 1,200 miles (1,900 km) from farms to shops, and eventually to your breakfast table. By buying food from local farmers' markets, your family can reduce the amount of greenhouse gas released from transporting foods.

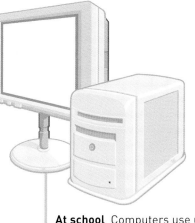

At school Computers use up to 70 percent less electricity if you put them to sleep instead of using a screensaver between classes, and 100 percent less when they are switched off at the end of the day.

Break time The last person out of a classroom can save several days' worth of electricity every year, just by turning off lights before leaving. And stocking a reusable lunchbox with locally bought foods makes your lunch more eco-friendly.

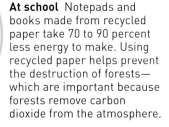

Getting to school During rush hour, half of all the cars on the road are driven by parents taking their children to school. If you walk or ride your bike to school, rather than riding in the car with your parents, you can save more than a ton of greenhouse gas per year.

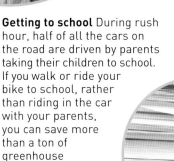

At school Notepads and books made from recycled paper take 70 to 90 percent less energy to make. Using recycled paper helps prevent the destruction of forests—which are important because forests remove carbon dioxide from the atmosphere.

What you can do at school

What you can do at home

Temperature Moving the thermostat down 2 degrees in winter and up 2 degrees in summer can save as much as 2 tons (2 t) of greenhouse gas each year. Using ceiling fans instead of air-conditioning in summer saves tons more.

Waste Composting food scraps and recycling containers cuts carbon dioxide emissions from manufacturing new materials, and methane emissions from garbage dumps. Recycling half your household waste can save 2,400 pounds (1,100 kg) of greenhouse gas per year.

Goodnight world Finally, switching off lights, computers, and other gadgets before bed might seem obvious, yet many people forget to do this. If you make the effort you can help save the planet while you sleep!

Paper

Cartons

Glass

Steel cans

Food scraps

Plastics

Aluminum

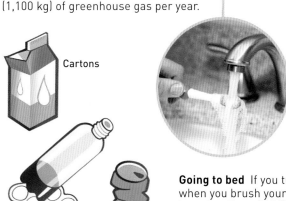

Going to bed If you turn off running water when you brush your teeth, you can save at least 2 gallons (7.6 l) of water each time you clean them, which adds up to 1,460 gallons (5,526 l) of water a year.

The future

What we do, right now, to tackle climate change could make a difference to the future of our planet. By reducing the amount of greenhouse gas we release, developing new technologies, and using renewable energy sources we can help stop global warming. In the end, it is up to all of us to protect the world we live in.

Start in your backyard The battle against climate change begins at home. We all need to do our part to save energy, recycle waste, and be aware of our carbon footprints on the world.

Use clean transport One day, hydrogen fuel that does not release any greenhouse gas may power our travel. Until then, we must develop cleaner, more efficient vehicles and fuels, and above all, use them.

Value the atmosphere
All life on Earth depends on the thin "skin" of gases that make up our atmosphere. From international cooperation to individual effort, we must work together to reduce the amount of greenhouse gas released around the world. We can choose to wait and do nothing, or we can act now and protect Earth's future.

Use renewable energy Instead of burning fossil fuels for power, we should develop and use renewable sources of energy, such as solar and wind power, that contribute much less greenhouse gas than fossil fuels. We need to start this work now, as new and clean renewable energies will take time to develop.

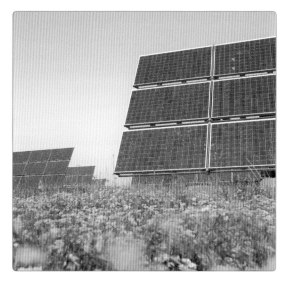

Protect forests We must act to protect our precious, carbon-trapping forests. Without the natural balance that trees provide, our efforts to reduce the carbon dioxide we release will be wasted.

Protect threatened species Reducing our greenhouse gas emissions will help protect threatened plants and animals, but we must also manage the damage that has already been done. We can do this by creating reserves and carefully managing our fishing, hunting, logging, and farming.

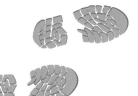

Glossary

Acid rain Highly acidic rainfall or snowfall, formed as nitrogen and sulfur oxides, are trapped in clouds.

Atmosphere A bubble of gases surrounding a planet. On Earth, this extends from the surface to about 6,000 miles (10,000 km) into space.

Biodegradable A term describing materials or substances that can be readily broken down by bacteria, insects, or other natural substances.

Biodiversity The number and variety of living species (including plants, animals, fungi, and bacteria) on Earth, or in a specific region.

Biofuel A fuel that is produced from biological sources, usually plants, rather than from fossil fuels.

Carbon dioxide (CO_2) A colorless, odorless gas formed when fuels and materials are burned, and by living organisms as they live, die, and rot.

Carbon footprint An estimate of the impact of one person's activities on the environment, measured by the amount of greenhouse gas released.

Carbon offsetting The act of balancing out the greenhouse gases released by a person or organization.

CFCs (Chlorofluorocarbons) Artificial chemicals used in air conditioners, refrigerators, and aerosol sprays, which damage the ozone layer and contribute to the greenhouse effect once released into the atmosphere.

Climate The weather that occurs in a region over a long period of time. The climate in a desert area, for example, is hot and dry.

Climate change A change in the world's climate and weather patterns, caused by sustained global warming.

Compact Fluorescent Lamp (CFL) A fluorescent lightbulb lined with phosphor, which uses much less energy than traditional lightbulbs.

Composting Converting food scraps, garden waste, or other organic materials into fertilizer by heaping leaves, wood chips, manure, or other materials on them to encourage the growth of bacteria.

Coral bleaching The loss of color in coral reefs that occurs as the algae that live in them are killed or forced out. Bleaching is linked to changes in sea temperature and acidity.

Desertification The process by which fertile land turns into desert as a result of changes to local climate and weather patterns, such as decreasing rainfall, as well as human activities.

Drought Long periods of extremely dry weather when little or no rain falls.

Eco-friendly Short for ecologically friendly—the name given to goods, materials, technology, or services thought to be harmless or relatively safe for the environment.

Emissions Substances released into the air by machines or natural processes—often used to describe gases released from engines and power stations.

Environment The physical and biological circumstances that surround us.

Fossil The remains, or traces, of any living thing preserved in, or as, rock.

Fossil fuels Carbon-based materials, such as oil, coal, and natural gas, formed from the fossils of ancient plants and animals. Fossil fuels are burned to produce energy and electricity.

Generator A machine that uses movement, usually from a spinning turbine, to make electricity.

Glacier A huge mass of ice formed from compacted snow, which slowly flows across land over thousands of years.

Global warming An observed increase in the average temperature of Earth's atmosphere, leading to climate change and other effects.

Green Party A political organization committed to protection of the environment and natural ecosystems.

Green technology Machines and processes developed to be less damaging to the environment than existing technologies.

Greenhouse effect The process by which gases in Earth's atmosphere trap solar radiation, absorbing it and bouncing it back to Earth to heat the atmosphere, oceans, and surface.

Greenhouse gases Gases in Earth's atmosphere that contribute to the greenhouse effect. Carbon dioxide (CO_2) makes up more than 99 percent of these gases.

Gray water Dirty water drained from baths, showers, dishwashers, or washing machines, which can be recycled in order to reduce water use at home.

Heat wave An extended period of extremely hot weather.

Hurricane A powerful storm that forms over warm, tropical waters, causing violent winds and rainstorms. Also known as a tropical cyclone.

Hybrid car Hybrid-electric vehicle that combines a standard internal combustion (gas) engine with a rechargeable, battery-powered electric motor.

Hydroelectric power A form of renewable energy, based on changing the movement of water into electricity. Dams capture river water and direct it past turbine generators at high speed.

Ice age Long periods of time in Earth's history when the climate was very cold and almost all of the planet was covered with ice and glaciers.

Ice cores Samples of ancient ice that scientists study to learn about Earth's atmosphere and climate in ancient times.

Industry The making of products, usually through the construction and use of machinery and factories.

Insulation Material used to surround an object, person, or house in order to reduce heat loss.

Kyoto Protocol An agreement between governments around the world that was created in 2005. It aims to limit or reduce greenhouse gas emissions to prevent climate change.

Landfill A dump site where waste is buried, forming piles or pits that release methane gas as they rot.

Malaria An infectious blood disease carried by mosquitoes, which kills thousands of people in tropical regions every year.

Methane An odorless, flammable gas formed by natural processes and living organisms. It is the main ingredient of natural gas and is one of the greenhouse gases in the atmosphere.

Nitrogen oxides Gases, most often released by vehicle exhausts, that contribute to both global warming and the formation of smog and acid rain.

Ozone layer The thin layer of ozone gas, located roughly 15 miles (24 km) above Earth's surface, that shields us from ultraviolet rays generated by the Sun.

Radiation Energy that moves as waves or rays. Solar radiation is the source of all our energy on Earth, and includes ultraviolet (UV) radiation, visible light, and infrared (or heat) radiation.

Recycle To keep, process, and reuse materials in order to save energy and reduce waste.

Reforestation Planting new trees to replace or restock forests.

Renewable energy Energy from sources that happen naturally, over and over again, and do not run out.

Solar power A form of renewable energy, based on changing radiation from the sun into electricity.

Tidal power A form of renewable energy, based on changing the movement of ocean tides into electricity.

Turbine A spinning wheel surrounded by blades, buckets, or cups, which helps change the energy from moving water or air into electricity.

Wave power A form of renewable energy, based on changing the movement of waves into electricity.

Wind power A form of renewable energy, based on changing the movement of wind into electricity, usually using windmill-like wind turbines.

Index

Credits

The publisher thanks Barbara Sheppard and Lachlan McLaine for their contributions, and Puddingburn for the index.

Photographs
Key t=top; l=left; r=right; tl=top left; tcl=top center left; tc=top center; tcr=top center right; tr=top right; cl=center left; c=center; cr=center right; b=bottom; bl=bottom left; bcl=bottom center left; bc=bottom center; bcr=bottom center right; br=bottom right

AAP = Australian Associated Press; CBT = Corbis; GI = Getty Images; iS = istockphoto.com; N_T = NASA/TOMS; N_V = NASA/Visible Earth; NOAO = National Optical Astronomy Observatory; PD = Photodisc; PL = photolibrary.com; SPL = Science Photo Library; SH = Shutterstock

Front cover GI; **back cover** b Gabrielle Green/iStock, tl Lionel Portier; **spine** Gabrielle Green.

4-5c GI; 5br iS; 6-7c PL; 8cl AAP; 9t GI; 10tr CBT; 11t GI; 12cr iS; 13cl CBT; 16bl, br, r, tr GI; cr iS; 17t GI; 19tc PD; 20-21c PL; 22bl GI; r SPL; 23l SPL; 24tr SH; 25r AAP; tl GI; 26tr AAP; 27cr, tr N_V; tl PL; 28-29b NOAO; tr AAP; 29tl CBT; tr AAP; 30cl AAP; 31t GI; 32bl CBT; br PL; cri iS; 33br SPL; 34br GI; bl SH; 35bl, br, c iS; tl GI; 36c GI; 38br GI; 39b, bcr, bl, br N_T; tl GI; tr AAP; 40tr SeaGen; 41bl iS; t AAP; 42c, cl PL; 44bl PL; 46br MP; tr CBT; 47cr SPL; t CBT; 48-49c iS; 50bl, c, cr iS; br AAP; 52-53c NASA; 53tcr iS; tr Ad-Libitum; 56b AAP; 58bc, br, c, tr iS; 59br, c, cl, cr, r, tc, tl, tr iS; 60cl, bl GI; c N_V; 61br GI; cr, tr iS.

Illustrations
Peter Bull Art Studio 14cl, 14-15c; **Andrew Davies/Creative Communication** 8b, 17, 27br, 46cl, 54-5c; **Chris Forsey** 11bcl, bcr, bl, br; **Malcolm Godwin** 43c; **Gabrielle Green** 41br; **Gabrielle Green/iStock** 1c, 32tr, 51c, 55br; **iStock** 8cr, 9c, 19tr, 43tc tcl; **Markus Junker** 40l; **David Kirshner** 34tr; **Lionel Portier** 12l, 23cr r; **Ken Rinkel** 8c, 9cl, 18c, 19tcr tl tr, 24bl, 25bl, 26bc, 30b, 31br, 35tr, 43tcr tr, 44bcr c, 47b, 55bc, 56tr, 57c, 59bc; **Michael Saunders** 10bcl, bcr, bl, br; **Spellcraft Studio e.K.** 33c.